WATSON
THE FINAL PROBLEM

Copyright © 2025 by Bert Coules and Tim Marriott

All rights reserved. No part of this publication may be reproduced or transmitted in any form or by any means, electronic or mechanical, including photocopying, recording or any information storage or retrieval system, without prior permission.

This play is available for performance by professional and amateur companies and individuals. For information regarding licencing and fees please contact Smokescreen Productions:

www.smokescreenprods.com

The right of Bert Coules and Tim Marriott to be identified as the authors of this work has been asserted by them in accordance with the Copyright Designs and Patents Act 1988.

First published in the United Kingdom in 2025 by
The Choir Press

ISBN: 978-1-78963-548-5

WATSON
THE FINAL PROBLEM

Watson. An old soldier with a few bruises and a cracking story to tell.

A one-act drama for a solo performer
by Bert Coules & Tim Marriott

Based on the stories of
Sir Arthur Conan Doyle

SMOKESCREEN PUBLICATIONS

HISTORY

The idea of a one-man play placing Dr John H Watson "in his rightful place front and centre" as one reviewer put it, came to actor Tim Marriott when he was on a family holiday to the most appropriate of locations: the village of Meiringen in Switzerland, which plays a vital part in Sir Arthur Conan Doyle's Sherlock Holmes stories and celebrates that fact with a museum and a striking statue of the sleuth.

Watson: The Final Problem was first performed at the Grove Theatre, Eastbourne in 2020. Original music was composed by Clive Whitburn and the sound design was by Bert Coules who also directed.

Since then, Tim has toured the same production to great acclaim and five-star reviews all over the UK and to Australia and the US, where it was part of the prestigious Brits off Broadway festival in New York.

TIM MARRIOTT

Tim Marriott is probably best known in the UK for seven series of BBC TV's leisure centre situation comedy The Brittas Empire, appearing in every episode as deputy manager Gavin. Other TV credits include British Airman Tigger Thompson in Allo Allo, Doctors, The Bill, An Actor's Life for Me, The Main Event, and Luv; and film credits include the forthcoming features The Real Thing, Revelation, and recently released comedy Love Type D. He returned to the stage in 2018 after a seventeen year 'career break' working in education.

In 2018 Tim toured Australia supporting the Invictus Games with his award-winning mental health themed solo show Shell Shock which was also performed at the Edinburgh and Adelaide Festivals where it won the Sunday Mail award, Best Solo Show, and also a Fringe Encore at SoHo Playhouse. Tim also wrote and produced another sell-out award-winning show on a Holocaust theme, Mengele. Watson: The Final Problem sold out shows at Edinburgh Festival Fringe in 2021 and 2022, where he won a Best Performance Award (Dark Chat). He also won an Edinburgh Festival Best Actor Award in 2023 for his new play Appraisal which sold out performances at Edinburgh and won a Best Theatre Award at Adelaide.

Besides producing and appearing in new theatre work around the world, Tim is also an experienced educator, voice-over artist, public speaker and event host. He delivers workshops on devising theatre and framing stories as well as keynote talks following Shell Shock performances, offering strategies for coping with anxiety, stress and trauma in partnership with Annabel Fen Marriott, an Anxiety UK practitioner and author of Toolkit for Anxiety.

Contact Tim Marriott at tm@smokescreenprods.com

BERT COULES

Bert Coules wandered through a succession of jobs including librarian, manager of a fringe opera company, audio engineer, and BBC producer-director before becoming a full-time writer. His work includes comedy, science fiction, horror, historical drama, and biographies but he is especially associated with crime and detective stories: he was the head writer on the BBC's unique project to dramatise the entire Sherlock Holmes canon, the first time it had ever been done with the same two actors in the leads throughout. The shows were a success and Bert was commissioned by the BBC to script four more series of brand-new cases for the detective and the doctor.

Beyond Baker Street, Bert has penned dramatisations of several of Ellis Peters' medieval Brother Cadfael mysteries, and of books by

Ursula Le Guin, Isaac Asimov, Ian Rankin, Alistair MacLean, Val McDermid and many others.

Stage works include an acclaimed version of Lost Empires, J B Priestley's coming-of-age novel about the decline of the music halls, as well as a full-length Holmes and Watson drama for two actors and a third who walks through a door, speaks one line, and promptly falls down dead.

Bert gives talks on the history of radio drama and on the Holmes and Watson stories, and has twice been invited to speak at the annual New York gathering of the international Baker Street Irregulars society, of which he is a proud member.

He is currently working on a screenplay for a new version of The Hound of the Baskervilles.

Contact Bert Coules at
www.bertcoules.co.uk

PRODUCTION GUIDELINES

The play is set in a room in Dr John Watson's house in Kensington, South London, in May 1894, but Watson's tale takes him and the audience to a variety of other locations and times. In the original production these were evoked solely by light and by sound to ensure an uninterrupted flow of scenes.

The set had a central armchair with a small table beside it, a desk with another chair, a hatstand, and a wooden crate which served as a hiding place for the items which Watson finds at the Reichenbach falls.

The only really essential props are a notebook, a book to represent Watson's novel The Sign of the Four, a box containing a revolver (or the weapon could be in a drawer if the desk has one), a silver cigarette case, a folded hand-written note, and a newspaper.

Not essential but providing a potentially moving point of focus is a framed photograph of Watson's late wife for his desk.

Other items are mentioned in the text and can be used, ignored, or added to, as desired.

Darkness.

Music.

Watson enters laboriously, supporting himself with a cane.

He sits, lit by a single spot.

WATSON: There was a power. A deep, organising power which pervaded London like a fog, which crept out of the very stones. A man who sat motionless like a spider at the centre of its web, but that web had a thousand radiations and he knew every quiver of each one of them.

He was the organiser of half that was evil and nearly all that was undetected in this great city. And he was unmasked by Sherlock Holmes. Hunted, tracked down, and named. Moriarty. The Napoleon of Crime.

The moment hangs.

The lights snap up.

No, no, that won't do. According to Holmes, I'm far too fond of telling my stories wrong end foremost. And I'm afraid it's true. Let me tell you how everything actually started.

Suddenly, the horror of battle. Screams, shouts, gunfire, horses. It's 1880 and Watson is a young and active man again.

Get that stretcher over here! These two to go back. No, leave him. Leave him! Keep pressure on that wound. Move, man! Get those men clear!

Louder than the general uproar, two rifle shots. Watson cries out and collapses.

He lies unmoving.

The battle fades and Watson gets up.

The war in Afghanistan brought honours and promotion to

many but for me it had nothing but misfortune and disaster. I took two bullets from a Jezail rifle. Filthy things. One in the leg, one in the shoulder. The bones were shattered. I would have fallen into the hands of the enemy but somehow Murray my orderly threw me across a pack-horse and got me safely back to the British lines. Brave man. Dead now.

I was worn and weary and sick of the sights that I'd seen. I came down with enteric fever. For a time my life was despaired of - and I despaired of life. Finally, weak and emaciated, I was despatched home. Six weeks at sea in an overcrowded troop ship and then I landed at Portsmouth with my health in ruins and my nerves in shreds. I was hardly able to help myself, never mind anyone else.

When you apply to medical school they ask you why you want to become a doctor. I told them I wanted to make a difference in the world, I wanted to be of use. That's what I was born to do, I told them. I was young and innocent and they'd heard it a thousand times before of course. But the fact was, I genuinely believed it. I really did think that one man could make a difference. And all through my training I still believed it - I was the very model of the idealistic young doctor.

Then after I qualified I joined the army and was despatched to India, to the north-west frontier - and I discovered that an Afghan bullet doesn't care how old you are, a bomb doesn't care about your lofty ideals, and a Khyber knife doesn't give a damn as it slits your throat.

I saw friends and comrades butchered in front of my eyes. And I grew up pretty fast, before those two bullets closed that particular chapter and sent me home.

The sounds of late 19th century London creep in.

So there I was. Back home. Naturally enough I gravitated

to London. That great cesspool that sucks in all the loungers and idlers of the Empire.

He looks around, taking in the sights and sounds of the city.

I stayed for some time at a private hotel in the Strand, leading a comfortless, meaningless existence and spending what little money I had much too freely. It was only when the state of my finances became genuinely alarming that I finally woke up to reality and realised I had to make a complete alteration to the way I was living. I made up my mind to leave the hotel and take up my quarters somewhere rather less pretentious and considerably less expensive.

And as fate would have it, it was on that very same day that I ran into an old colleague from Bart's Hospital. Young Stamford. By God, it was a pleasant thing to a lonely man to find a friendly face in the great, grey wilderness. I took him off to lunch - hang the expense! - and told him I was looking for comfortable lodgings at an affordable price. He laughed.

I got rather short with him scoffing at my new-found resolution and I demanded to know just what was so damned amusing about it. 'Sorry,' he said, 'but you're the second man today who's said those very words to me. The other chap's found his comfortable rooms all right but the rent's too much for his pocket and he can't persuade anyone to go halves'.

Well, that threw a different light on things. I was the very man for him! I told Stamford I'd prefer sharing with someone to being on my own - as long as he was studious and quiet and easy to get on with.

Stamford looked at me rather strangely over his wine glass. 'You don't know him yet,' he said.

The quiet atmosphere of Bart's Hospital.

It did my heart good to be back at Bart's. History, tradition, memories. I had some very happy -

The background cuts abruptly.

And suddenly - there he was. Stamford introduced us. 'Doctor Watson - Mr Sherlock Holmes.' Holmes greeted me cordially, asked me how I was, and shook my hand with a strength I'd hardly have given him credit for. Then he said, 'You've been in Afghanistan, I perceive'. I was astonished. I asked him how on earth he knew. He chuckled to himself. 'Never mind,' he said.

Well, I dare say you know most of the rest. You know about the science of deduction and detection, the cases, the clients, the triumphs, the way Scotland Yard's finest used to call at our rooms in Baker Street asking for his help. You're familiar with the chemical experiments in the sitting-room, the indoor target practice, the tobacco in the slipper, the unanswered letters stabbed to the mantelpiece with a jack-knife. The cocaine.

And if you'll forgive me a moment of immodesty, it's thanks to me that you know these things. John H Watson, companion, comrade, best-selling author, biographer, chronicler... friend. I like to think that, friend.

And now, it falls to me to tell you something that you don't know. Sherlock Holmes is dead.

Holmes died on the 4th of May, 1891. Yes, that's right: almost exactly three years ago to the very day. And you're wondering, I imagine, how can it be that you didn't hear at the time. No newspaper headlines, no obituary, no announcement of a funeral, no tributes, nothing. Nothing. It's true that he wasn't as famous then as he became later, but even so - I wondered myself, at first. And then I realised.

Holmes had a brother. Mycroft. Seven years his senior.

Holmes told me that Mycroft holds a junior office in the civil service, auditing the books for some of the government departments. Well, I believed him, of course - until I actually met the man. Imagine. Imagine Sherlock Holmes' mind, his sharpness, his intellect, his insights into the darkest depths of men's souls, his sheer... oddness. Imagine all that, magnified, intensified, even more disturbing. And I was supposed to believe that such a man 'audits the books'? One look at his eyes and I knew that there was far more to Mycroft Holmes than that. And when, three years ago, nothing appeared in the papers, I did some deducing of my own. Who else could have been responsible?

But I'm digressing and I apologise. I'm putting it off. Holmes was fond of saying that all I cared about in my stories was the drama, the colour, the sweep of the investigation, the thrill of the chase. What he wanted was clinical accounts full of cold hard facts: analysis, logic, details, science.

Look, take The Speckled Band. Do you remember that one? They were a young woman's dying words. The speckled band. There was no visible cause of death and her body was found in a sealed bedroom. Her sister came to Baker Street, shaking in terror of her life. What a case!

Disturbing darkness falls.

The locked door and windows, the mysterious noises in the night, the vigil in the dark, the low whistle, Holmes exploding into action: 'Do you see it Watson? Do you see it! The band! The speckled band!'.

He swipes furiously at the air with his cane. A snake hisses.

It was a snake. A swamp adder. The deadliest snake in India. Holmes thrashed at the creature and drove it back, back through the vent into the next room - where it turned in rage on its handler.

Muffled, a horrible dying scream.

He was dead in seconds. The girls' step father. The killer killed.

The lights come back up.

Holmes wanted me to call that story 'An analytical account of the Roylott-Stoner inheritance case with particular notes upon the training and employment of reptiles as murder weapons'. I ask you. Yes, I know, I'm still not getting to the real point. But allow me one more digression, if you will. It is a relevant one this time. Holmes introduced me to a world I scarcely knew existed. An endless parade of villains, policemen, murderers, blackmailers. Clients. One particular client.

Miss Mary Morstan was seven and twenty. A sweet, dainty, fragile creature, with soft blue eyes that were beautifully spiritual and sympathetic, even in the face of personal tragedy and fear.

He picks up a book.

Holmes raised his eyebrows when I showed him what I wrote about her later, but I stood by it then and I stand by it now.

He finds a page and reads:

'In an experience of women which extends over many nations and three separate continents, I had never looked upon a face which gave a clearer promise of a refined and sensitive nature.'

I did what I always did, I offered to leave her alone with Holmes so that she could talk in confidence. And she asked me to stay.

He holds up the book.

'The Sign of the Four'. It's all in there.

Miss Morstan's father had vanished twelve years earlier.

But that wasn't why she came to us. Every year since, on the anniversary of his disappearance, she had received an anonymous gift: a single pearl. And even that wasn't the reason. This year, there was something new.

He finds another page and reads:

'Be at the third pillar from the left outside the Lyceum Theatre to-night at seven o'clock. If you are distrustful, bring two friends. You are a wronged woman, and shall have justice. Do not bring police. Your unknown friend.'

This had arrived that very morning. 'A pretty little mystery' Holmes called it. I won't tell you the whole story. If you're interested, well then please buy the book. But I will tell you this: that case took me from the glamour of London's West End to a filthy attic in the suburbs, from a run-down shop full of stuffed animals to the bustle and noise of the docks, and from the cosiest, most loving home to a deadly boat chase along the Thames.

A man lay dead. Paralysed, with his face twisted in fear. The killer had escaped though the attic and across the roof. And it was in that attic, clear and awesome in the dust on the floor, that I discovered a vital clue. A single footprint. Naked - and tiny.

He is back there. He looks up, horrified.

'Holmes. A child has done this terrible thing.'

The truth turned out to be even stranger. A story that began in India many years before, a tale of trust and betrayal, of vengeance and death. Of wealth. Untold wealth. And of something else.

Love is a wondrous, subtle thing. In the midst of a terrifying business, as dark and as dreadful as any we'd encountered, my heart went out to her and hers to me. But I was still weak, still far from well, a man with no prospects and no more than a half-pay army pension to support myself. And thanks to Holmes - thanks to us - a fabulous lost treasure was found and Mary Morstan was an heiress, one of the richest women in the realm. What right had I even to look at her?

And then we all gathered, the treasure chest was opened - and it was empty. The thief, knowing he was about to be caught, had scattered the whole lot into the Thames. Jewels, pearls, gold, silver - all lost for ever. And I breathed, 'Thank God'.

She looked at me. She knew why I'd said it, I could see it in her face, in those wonderful eyes. But I had to put it into words. 'I said Thank God,' I told her, 'because now I'm free to tell you that I love you, Mary. I love you as truly as a man ever loved a woman'. Her reply is etched in my memory. 'In that case - my dear John - I say Thank God too.'

All this is by way of explaining why I'd moved out of the Baker Street rooms and was living here, in Kensington. A married man with a new medical practice of my own. I hadn't seen Holmes for quite some time, though of course I'd been following his activities in the papers. I knew that he was abroad on some delicate mission for the French government - which is why it came as something of a shock that late evening when he suddenly burst unannounced into my consulting room.

He edged his way along the wall, slammed the shutters on the window and bolted them. He looked terrible, thinner and paler than ever, and his knuckles were raw and bleeding. He tried to light a cigarette but his hands were shaking so much I had to do it for him. I'd rarely seen Sherlock Holmes in fear of anything but by God he was scared then. 'Air guns,' he said. 'I'm frightened of air guns.'

Air guns? What the devil could he possibly mean? I made him sit down, I poured him a drink and I dressed his hand. Eventually he pulled himself back to something more like his usual self and apologised for calling so late. Then he asked if he could leave by scrambling over the back wall of my garden.

What was all this about? He turned to me, as serious as I'd ever seen him, and asked if Mary was in. I told him she was away on a visit and he nodded. 'Good, that makes it easier. Watson, will you come away with me to the continent?' 'The continent? Where?' 'Oh, anywhere. It's all the same to me.' The man I knew would never propose a holiday, let alone an aimless one. He saw my expression, he pulled himself to his feet and he roamed the room. I waited.

'You've probably never heard of Professor Moriarty. No? No. No. And there's the genius and the wonder of the thing! No-one has heard of him. That's what puts him on a pinnacle in the records of crime. His life has been extraordinary. Good birth, excellent education - he held the Chair in Mathematics at one of the smaller universities. But he had hereditary tendencies of the most diabolical kind. A criminal strain ran in his blood. Dark rumours gathered around him in the university town, and eventually he was forced to resign his chair and to come down to London. Those are the public facts. That's what the world knows. And that is all the world knows!'

'For years now in every kind of case - robberies, forgeries, abductions, blackmail, murder, scandals, scandals reaching to the very highest in society - I've felt this malign presence. For years I struggled to break through the veil that surrounds it and shields it, and at last the time came. I saw the thread, I seized it and followed it and it led me through a thousand cunning twists and windings - straight to Moriarty'.

'He's a genius, Watson. A philosopher, an abstract thinker.

He's a true master of his art. He commits no crimes himself: he delegates, he issues his orders and they're passed down through all the layers of his organisation. Only those agents at the very top have direct contact with the man at the apex of the pyramid. I had all the evidence but he was so ringed around with protection that I couldn't move against him. I'd woven my net but couldn't pull it tight. And then he made a slip. Just one tiny slip but it was enough. I went to Scotland Yard. Oh, I had a hard time making them believe me but I succceded in the end. And together we laid our plans: separate simultaneous swoops on every level of the organisation, timed to the second so no warning can be given.

In three days the Professor, with all the principal members of his gang, will be in the hands of the police. And I had done all this in the most profound and desperate secrecy. One hint of what was planned, one minute vibration in that massive web, and all my months of effort would have been for nothing.

The lights dim. A violin plays. A clock ticks.

'Then, this morning I was in our old rooms in Baker Street, playing to concentrate my mind and going over the plans - when the door opened.

'It was him. The very man himself, standing on my threshold. His appearance was quite familiar to me. He's extremely tall and thin, his forehead domes out in a white curve. When he's deep in thought he has a habit of slowly oscillating his head from side to side. It makes him look curiously reptilian and repugnant. We exchanged... pleasantries and he produced a memorandum book.

'You crossed my path on the 4th of January. On the 23rd you incommoded me; by the middle of February I was seriously inconvenienced by you; at the end of March I was absolutely hampered in my plans; and now, at the close of

April, I find myself placed in such a position through your continual persecution that I am in positive danger of losing my liberty.

'You must drop it, Mr Holmes, you really must, you know. You hope to place me in the dock. I tell you that I will never stand in the dock. You hope to beat me. I tell you that you will never beat me. If you are clever enough to bring destruction upon me, rest assured that I shall do exactly the same to you.'

A still moment of his snake-like stare. Then he turns away.

The atmosphere returns to normal.

Holmes had been shaken by the confrontation: he tried to hide it but I knew him far too well. And he was right to be concerned. He told me that not an hour later he went out and a two-horse van drove furiously straight at him. He only saved himself by a second. Two other attacks followed in quick succession and then he was assaulted in an open street by a rough with a cudgel. 'I knocked him down, Watson, and the police have him, but I can tell you that absolutely no connection will ever be traced between him and the former professor of mathematics. No connection whatsoever!

'But I shall have him, Doctor, I shall have him! Then will come the greatest criminal trial of the century, and the rope for all of them. I tell you my friend it will go down as the finest bit of thrust-and-parry work in the entire history of detection!'

It was a fantastic story. And he was asking me to go off with him to God knows where? Holmes was not a man to run away from a confrontation and no more was I. I'd be lying if I said I didn't have my doubts about the whole thing. The life he led - wasn't it enough to take its toll on the strongest of men? To unseat even the surest of brains? Holmes was in a more frantic state than I'd ever seen him.

I asked him again, why did we have to go abroad? He told me the plans were so well laid he didn't need to be there for the actual arrests. Getting away, getting out of the country was the obvious - the necessary! - thing for him to do, he said. He was practically begging me to go with him. And I agreed. What choice did I have? The man obviously needed my help and I wasn't about to turn my back on him.

I pressed him to stay the night but he wasn't having it. 'It's too dangerous for you,' he said. He gave me instructions that I had to follow to the letter. 'To the letter! You are now playing against the cleverest rogue and the most powerful syndicate of criminals in Europe!'

(*Sighs*) Those instructions. I had to send my luggage - the barest minimum - to Victoria station that evening. And in the morning I had to take a hansom cab - but not the first or the second which came along, but the third. It had to be the third. I had to drive, not to the station but to the Strand end of the Lowther Arcade, and I must on no account tell the driver the destination but hand him a piece of paper with it written down. Holmes saw my reaction to that, but I don't think it registered - that was the clearest sign of all that he was far from his usual self.

'Time yourself,' he said, 'to get to the other end of the Arcade at exactly a quarter past nine. There'll be a small coach waiting, driven by a fellow wearing a heavy black cloak tipped at the collar with red. Don't speak a word to him, just get in. You'll arrive at Victoria just in time for the Dover Continental Express. A compartment will be reserved for us in the second first-class carriage from the front; I'll meet you there.'

Before I could say a word, he was gone. Through the window, over the garden wall and away into the night.

Well, I reached Victoria station by that remarkable route - and everything happened just as Holmes said it would. I collected my bag and found what was supposed to be our reserved compartment. It was occupied by a venerable Italian priest, who was trying in broken English to make a porter understand that his luggage was to be booked through to Paris. There was no sign of Holmes. I opened the window and stared vainly down the platform. The train was about to depart.

A chill of fear came over me. Then I heard a voice from behind me. 'My dear Watson. You haven't even condescended to say hello.' Yes, it was him. The old priest. I began to laugh with sheer relief but he silenced me with a glance and dropped his voice to a whisper. 'They're hot on our trail!'

Whistles and steam as the train pulls out.

'Yes! And there! There's the man himself!'

I looked out and saw a tall figure pushing his way through the crowd but he was too late, the train had already begun to move.

I had a great deal to think about as the train weaved its smoky way through the Kentish countryside.

The train clatters along. Time passes.
A sudden burst of steam and activity as the train pulls to a stop.

We arrived at Canterbury. Holmes suddenly pulled me to my feet and pushed me out onto the platform. The train pulled away, taking my bag and my clothes with it. I demanded to know what the devil he was about.

'I tell you, Moriarty's brain is quite on a level with mine. He's done what I would do in his place. Having missed our express he's arranged a special private train to follow ours. There's always a delay at Dover and he'll plan on catching us there.'

This was verging on the ridiculous and I told him so. It

takes time to engage a special. The engine has to be found and so does at least one coach. The line has to be cleared, people have to be informed. Holmes shrugged it off. 'I tell you he'll do it.

A distant whistle grows as a train approaches.

'He will do it. Quick, man! Get down!'

The train thunders past, steam hissing, whistle blasting.

That train was moving faster than any I'd ever seen. And at one window, a chilling face scanning the platform with cold, malevolent eyes. It was the man I'd seen at Victoria. It was Moriarty. Holmes looked shrewdly at me. 'Any more doubts about my mental stability, Doctor'. No, I hadn't. Of course I hadn't. But good grief, had I really been so transparent? He smiled. 'Only to me. No, not another word. Come on, my friend.'

On to Dover? I said. 'No. We'll throw him off our trail, and he'll have to return to London empty-handed.'

We made our way cross-country to Newhaven, and then over to Dieppe, treating ourselves to a couple of carpet-bags and new necessities as we went. We reached Brussels that same night and the next day moved on to Strasburg. Then Monday dawned - the day of the police raids.

Holmes telegraphed Scotland Yard and the answer arrived the same evening. Holmes tore it open and then with a bitter curse hurled it into the fire. 'He's escaped. They've got all the principal agents but he gave them the slip. Incompetent fools! You'll find me a dangerous companion now, Watson. Moriarty will devote his whole energies to tracking us down and revenging himself upon me. I think you'd better return to England.'

He must have known how I'd react to that. I pointed out that I was an old campaigner as well as an old friend. I'd never let him down when danger was near and I had no intention of starting then. We argued about it for a good half-hour - and then I had my way. I can be every bit as stubborn as Sherlock Holmes if the need arises.

That same evening we resumed our journey, heading for Geneva. From there we wandered up the Valley of the Rhone, and then branching off at Leuk, made our way towards the Gemmi Pass, still deep in snow. In the homely Alpine villages and the lonely mountains, Holmes' quick glancing eyes took in every face that passed us. But we saw no sign of the danger which dogged our footsteps.

But he was never depressed: in fact I'd rarely seen him in such exuberant spirits. I knew why, of course: he was relishing the situation, however dangerous it might be. Never for one instant did he forget the shadow which lay across him, but he was on a case, the game was afoot, and nothing else mattered. It was what he lived for.

And I won't lie to you: I felt it too. God knows, I loved my life in London: my wife, my work, my friends - but there in those mountains, far from anything familiar and safe, facing danger with Sherlock Holmes at my side... I'm not ashamed to admit it: I'd rarely felt so alive.

Mountain wind.

Before tackling the Gemmi Pass we paused at a wayside shelter where we met a small group of travellers complete with a local guide and pack ponies. I was grateful for their company: the views from the Pass were spectacular but it wasn't a trip for the faint-hearted: some passages weren't much more than narrow ledges cut into the cliffs, with chains to cling on to.

I don't think Holmes ever touched them: lost in thought and with his steps never faltering, he seemed to be mesmerised by the sight of the distant mountains. I'd never before seen him so absorbed in the beauties and mysteries of nature.

We were walking along the border of the melancholy Daubensee lake when suddenly we heard a noise almost directly above us. A massive rock flew down across the path and into the lake.

A huge boulder crashes down and splashes into the water.

Holmes raced up to a ridge and craned his neck in every direction. But if he saw anything he never mentioned it. The mountain guide assured us that this sort of thing was common at that particular spot, but Holmes smiled quietly at me with the air of a man whose expectations had at last been fulfilled.

The Gemmi Pass took us to Interlaken where we bade farewell to our new companions. Then we pressed on, alone once more.

Swiss village atmosphere.

It was on the 3rd of May that we reached the charming little village of Meiringen, where we put up at the Englischer Hof hotel. Our landlord, Peter Steiler, was an intelligent man, and spoke excellent English, having served for three years as a waiter at the Grosvenor Hotel in London. Holmes deduced this without needing to be told. Steiler was amazed, as most people were when Holmes pulled information seemingly out of mid-air. 'But this is unglaublich! Doctor, he is a mind-reader!'

Holmes smiled back at him, basking in the praise as he always did. He soaked up applause as avidly as any prima donna. 'Only at the Grosvenor could you have learned the recipe for tonight's splendid fricandeau of veal, Herr Steiler. Monsieur Romarque's sauce is quite unmistakeable. I must say, I'm surprised he revealed it to you.'

Our host grinned. 'He was my very good friend!' And we

laughed, all three of us laughed. Steiler beamed. 'Oh, this is good, is it not? To hear you laugh so in my hotel, it makes me content. You are content also? Herr Holmes?'

'Yes, Herr Steiler. I am content.'

Evening falls.

It was a magical evening. We sat on the terrace with our fine Swiss beer and gazed at the magnificent view in the evening sunshine. You could see two seasons at a single glance: spring at the foot of the mountains and winter at their peaks. I told Holmes I'd like to bring Mary here. Her health hadn't been too good just lately. He was immediately concerned, but I reassured him: it was nothing serious, I said, nothing to worry about. And this place, that view - it would work wonders for her.

Holmes was in one of his philosophical moods. He had said to me more than once that he would have made a formidable criminal and I believed him, but I wasn't prepared for what he told me that night: that in Moriarty he saw the man that he could have become.

'It's true, Doctor. I can see into his mind, I know what drives him and I understand it completely. There's a beauty to mathematics. It's the quest to impose order and logic and clarity onto a chaotic world. We both follow that quest, Moriarty and I. If his path is by embracing evil and mine by combatting it, that's a small enough difference among so many similarities.'

Did Holmes know about the very latest medical thinking? The shadow, the dark, buried part of the self that constantly strives to be recognised. It was my belief that Holmes *embraced* his shadow, he used its power to channel his vitality and creativity into solving mysteries.

He somehow only became fully alive when he had a case. And when there was nothing to occupy his brain, then there came the black depressions, the day-long silences, the drugs. The shadow at work, the duality suddenly made clear. Moriarty, though, was a slave to his shadow, it had consumed him. Dense, deep and destructive, it owned his very soul. The man was all shadow, and like a shadow he was following us.

Evening turns to night.

We sat there as the dusk turned to night and the stars began to appear, each of us lost in his own private thoughts. And then, so softly that I almost didn't notice, Holmes spoke again. 'I think, Watson, I might say that I've not lived wholly in vain. If my record were closed tonight I could survey it with equanimity. The air of London is the sweeter for my presence. In over a thousand cases I'm not aware that I have ever used my powers on the wrong side. And now I face the most dangerous and capable criminal in Europe. Your memoirs will draw to an end on the day that I crown my career by terminating his activities.'

This was something entirely unexpected. I asked him if he really planned to retire. I will never forget his reply and the way he said it. 'My... retirement would be a price I'd willingly pay.'

The night fades. Morning dawns.

The next day we decided to follow Peter Steiler's advice and take the long walk to see the fabled waterfalls of Reichenbach.

The awesome roar of the falls.

It is a fearful place. The torrent, swollen by the melting snow, plunges past glistening coal-black rocks into a tremendous chasm, and as the long sweep of green water roars forever down, the spray rolls up like the smoke from a burning house. We stood on a narrow path near the edge, peering down at the gleam of the breaking water far below us and listening to the half-human shout which came booming up with the spray out of the abyss.

Holmes turned to me. 'Look at it. A man could spend his life probing the secrets of such a power. This will stretch your pen, Watson. It's a worthy subject for your prose'. I was surprised. 'No sarcasm, Holmes? No comments about cheap romanticism and pandering to the masses?' He shook his head. 'Oh no, my friend. Not here. Not today.'

As we made our way back to more secure ground we saw a young Swiss lad running towards us with a note in his hand. It was from Peter Steiler and it was addressed to me. An English lady had arrived at the hotel and was deathly ill having suffered a sudden catastrophic haemorrhage. Steiler believed that that she could scarcely last a few more hours and it would surely be a great comfort to her to see an English doctor. Could I return?

I don't think I've ever been so torn between the bonds of friendship and my duty as a doctor. The note was genuine, it was on the hotel's paper, so there was no doubting the situation and the urgency, but how could I leave Holmes on his own, knowing the danger?

He saw my struggle and resolved the question himself: he suggested that the young Swiss messenger could remain with him as guide and companion while I returned to Meiringen. My friend would stay some little time at the falls, he said, and would then walk slowly over the hill to the next village, where I could catch up with him later.

As I hurried away I turned back briefly. Holmes was standing with his back against a rock and his arms folded, gazing down at the rush of the waters.

The falls give way to the village.

It must have been a little over an hour before I reached Meiringen. Old Steiler was standing at the porch of his hotel.

'I trust she's no worse?' I said. A look of surprise passed over his face, and my heart turned to lead. I didn't wait for any explanations.

Back to the falls.

I cursed my damn leg as I tried to hurry, and for all my efforts it took me nearly two hours to climb back up to the falls. (*Yells*) 'Holmes! Holmes! Holmes!

(*To himself*) 'Calm down. Think. Think! He's gone on to the village just as we planned. He'll be waiting there - (*Seeing something*) Oh God. God.' Holmes' stick was still leaning on the rock where I'd last seen him.

'Holmes!'

I was cold and sick with the horror of the thing but then I thought of Holmes' own methods and tried to apply them. It was all too easy to do. In the damp black soil I could make out fresher footprints than ours from earlier. One set moving lightly away back down the path - that must have been the Swiss lad. And a heavier, more deliberate track.

Someone new had approached Holmes while I wasn't there. And then the two of them had moved off together. Along the path to the edge of the falls.

Two men had made their way there. Neither had returned. And the ground at the very brink of the precipice was churned and gouged.

'Dear God, they must have fought hand-to-hand. Holmes! Holmes…'

The falls slowly fade, under:

Suddenly, the gleam of something caught my eye. It was Holmes' silver cigarette case lying on a rock.

Watson retrieves it.

And something was trapped beneath it. I was destined to have a last word from my friend and comrade. The writing was as firm and precise as if he'd been at his desk in Baker Street.

(*He reads*) 'My dear Watson. I write these few lines through the courtesy of Mr Moriarty, who awaits my convenience for the final discussion of those questions which lie between us. I am pleased to think that I shall be able to free society from any further effects of his presence, though I fear that it will be at a cost which will give pain to my friends, and especially, my dear Watson, to you.

'I have already explained to you, however, that no possible conclusion to my career could be more congenial to me than this. Indeed, if I may make a full confession to you, I was quite convinced that the letter from Meiringen was a hoax.

'I made every disposition of my property before leaving England, and handed it to my brother Mycroft. Pray give my greetings to Mrs Watson, and believe me to be, my dear fellow, very sincerely yours, Sherlock Holmes.'

It was impossible to recover the bodies. There, in that dreadful cauldron of swirling water and seething foam, will lie for all time the most dangerous criminal and the foremost champion of the law of their generation.

A solo violin plays, echoing and unreal. We are back in Watson's home.

The powers of fate rarely pay heed to mere mortal men. Holmes knew that. Not six months after I returned from Switzerland, I suddenly realised that Mary - my kind, gentle, lovely, loving wife Mary - was far more ill than either of us had realised. And I - I could do nothing.

I had to sit at her bedside and watch her simply being...

taken away from me. At the end, as I was holding her hand, she managed to open her eyes and speak. It was scarcely more than a breath. 'Oh, John. First Mr Holmes and now me. Everyone you love. I'm so very sorry.' She apologised. Apologised. And then she was gone. And I was alone again.

I was at my lowest ebb since I'd arrived back home from Afghanistan years before, half dead and with no hope of any future. No, this was worse, far worse. I'd seen that future, I'd lived it, I'd gloried in it. And now it had been stolen and could never come back.

He opens a box and produces a gun.

My old service revolver. A souvenir, and not just of my time in the army. This had been a friend to me far more recently than that. Some of the dangers we'd faced... And I still had some bullets. Yes, I considered it. Dear Lord, I really did. Came close, too.

Calmly, he contemplates the weapon. Then with shocking speed and determination he raises it to his head.

A long frozen moment. Then:

'Honestly, Watson, is it really necessary to be quite so melodramatic?'

He lowers the gun.

He was still in my head. Thank God. And so was Mary, of course. I could suddenly see the look on her face, the disappointment, the anger. And I was furious too, furious with myself. Was this the man she fell in love with? No it was not.

He puts the gun away.

I tried to lose myself in my work, but my practice had never been particularly absorbing even in happier days and I found that nothing had changed. I still had stories to write, of course. I decided that if Mycroft Holmes hadn't wanted his brother's death to be public knowledge he must have had a damn good reason, so no-one was going to learn about it from me. I kept writing. I was cagey about dates and times without ever actually lying about things. And I would have carried on too, until I finally ran out of material, but then just recently my hand was forced.

He picks up a newspaper.

A letter to the Times. Demanding a full and immediate official enquiry into the disappearance of Professor James Moriarty. (*He reads*) 'Sir. I call upon the Home Secretary and the Commissioner of Police to provide urgent and public explanations.

'I have long had documented evidence of the prolonged persecution of this respected and highly distinguished scientist and academic by the self-styled 'consulting detective' Mr Sherlock Holmes, but now there has come into my possession irrefutable proof of the Professor's cold-blooded murder by the same hand.'

There have been several more on the same lines, you might have seen them. All from Moriarty's brother. He's an army man, a colonel, and if you ask me he's a damned disgrace to the rank. I'm not having this. The rumours have already started, the loose assumptions, the false stories. Soon there'll come the scandal-mongering, the out-and-out lies, the headlines designed purely to sell the papers, those rags. It's damn near impossible sometimes to tell facts from falsehood. What's happened to the world?

So - I've decided to take matters into my own hands and the hell with any consequences. I alone know the truth and I mean to see that truth told. The account's written and I'm sending it to the Strand Magazine tomorrow. And that will be that. I've decided that I shan't write up any more cases. It wouldn't be... respectful. Let the poor man rest in peace. Here...

He reads from a notebook.

'In an incoherent and, as I deeply feel, an entirely inadequate fashion, I have tried to give some account of my many strange experiences in the company of the world's first, and only, private consulting detective. But now, with a heavy heart, I lay down my pen. These have been the last words in which I shall ever record the singular gifts of my friend Mr Sherlock Holmes, whom I shall ever regard as the best and the wisest man whom I have ever known.'

And there it is. The Final Problem. Not a bad title, perhaps, for the final story. No more Sherlock Holmes for me. No more Sherlock Holmes for anyone. Still, we had a damn good run.

So - what now, eh? What does the world hold for John H Watson MD, late of the Fifth Northumberland Fusiliers? I've been doctor, soldier, husband, detective - what's next?

Well, if I've learned anything at all from my long association with Mr Sherlock Holmes it's this: always expect the unexpected. There might be something wonderful, something incredible, just around the corner.

Off, a doorbell jangles.

Ha! You see?

He readies himself. Off, footsteps approach up the stairs.

A knock at the door.

Watson stands tall and smiles, a man renewed.

Come in!

Closing music.

THE END

ACKNOWLEDGEMENTS

Cover design by Bert Coules

Cover image of Tim Marriott by Peter Mould

On stage images by Orion Powell

Bert Coules headshot by Albane of Sandgate

www.ingramcontent.com/pod-product-compliance
Lightning Source LLC
LaVergne TN
LVHW051513070426
835507LV00022B/3088